I0182182

Why Iran Is Unraveling

Protest, Repression, and the Crisis of Power

By Roozbeh Mirebrahimi

Free Quill

Copyright@ 2026 Roozbeh Mirebrahimi
All rights reserved.

ISBN: 9780985374846
Publisher: Free Quill
Non-Stop Media, Inc.
New York, USA

Price: $ 10.00

Dedicated to the beautiful souls
who sacrificed themselves for freedom

Table of Contents

Prelude

December 2025: The Last Warning Before Collapse

The protests of December 2025 did not begin with an announcement, a manifesto, or a carefully coordinated political plan. They began, instead, in a place long associated with economic pulse rather than street rebellion: Tehran's Grand Bazaar.[1] The initial spark came from shopkeepers and traders protesting the rapid collapse of the national currency, runaway inflation, and what they openly described as the economic breakdown of the Islamic Republic. Their anger was not ideological. It was transactional, immediate, and existential. The market, once a pillar of economic stability and regime accommodation, was signaling that the system could no longer sustain itself.

From there, protests spread quickly and unevenly. Early demonstrations appeared both in commercial districts and in scattered urban and peripheral areas, reflecting a society already

---

[1] Tehran Grand Bazaar — One of the oldest and most influential commercial centers in Iran, the Tehran Grand Bazaar has long functioned as more than a marketplace. Historically, it has been a critical social and political space where merchants (*bazaaris*), clerics, and informal networks intersect. During key moments of modern Iranian history—most notably the Constitutional Revolution (1905–1911), the 1979 Revolution, and later periods of political unrest—bazaar closures, strikes, and collective actions signaled serious challenges to state authority. The bazaar's economic leverage, rooted in trade, credit, and supply chains, has repeatedly allowed it to amplify popular discontent and transform economic protest into broader political pressure.

primed for unrest. As in previous uprisings, there was no single triggering policy that could explain the scale of the reaction. What transformed localized protests into a nationwide wave was a shared recognition that the economic crisis was no longer cyclical or manageable—it was structural and irreversible. December 2025 marked the moment when economic collapse was no longer feared, but felt.

At first, the uprising resembled earlier waves: decentralized, leaderless, and driven by accumulated rage rather than coordinated strategy. But this time, a crucial new element entered the equation. As protests escalated, the public call by Prince Reza Pahlavi[2]—who in recent years had emerged as one of the most visible symbols of opposition—played a decisive role in transforming the movement. For the first time in many years, a large segment of protesters felt that the uprising was not only an expression of rejection, but also connected to a recognizable figure offering political direction and a future-oriented narrative.

This intervention did not create the protests, but it altered their trajectory. Many demonstrators had long known what they opposed: the current system, its corruption, its repression, and its economic ruin. What had been missing was a shared sense of what might come next. The call from Pahlavi, framed around national unity,

---

[2] Reza Pahlavi — Son of Mohammad Reza Shah Pahlavi, the last monarch of Iran, Reza Pahlavi has lived in exile since the 1979 Revolution. Over the past decades, he has emerged as a prominent opposition figure advocating for a secular, democratic transition in Iran through nonviolent means. While he does not claim a formal political role or seek restoration of the monarchy, Pahlavi has positioned himself as a unifying national figure, emphasizing popular sovereignty, a future referendum on Iran's system of governance, and the separation of religion and state. His statements and interventions have often gained renewed attention during periods of nationwide protest, particularly as a symbol of continuity with a pre–Islamic Republic political order and as a focal point for segments of the Iranian diaspora.

democratic transition, and a post–Islamic Republic horizon, provided something unprecedented in recent protest cycles: a provisional sense of leadership and an articulated alternative. For a movement historically defined by negation, this represented a qualitative shift. It was precisely this shift that triggered the regime's most violent response.

The state reacted with speed and brutality that exceeded even the benchmarks set in November 2019[3] and 2022.[4] Security and military forces moved decisively to crush the uprising before it could

---

[3] November 2019 protests in Iran — In mid-November 2019, a sudden government decision to sharply increase fuel prices sparked mass demonstrations across Iran's cities and towns beginning on 15 November. What started as protests against the steep hike quickly expanded into nationwide unrest expressing broader grievances over political repression, economic hardship, and systemic corruption. Security forces responded with lethal force, live ammunition, and heavy crackdown measures as protests spread to more than 100 cities. A near-total internet blackout was imposed for nearly a week, severely limiting communications and obstructing independent reporting. Human rights organizations documented hundreds of deaths (with estimates varying widely) and thousands of arrests in one of the most severe crackdowns in Iran since 1979, though the true toll remains contested due to state suppression of information. The events are often called "Bloody November" (Aban 98 in the Iranian calendar) and have continued to shape Iranian protest movements and debates over accountability.

[4] Nationwide protests in 2022 in Iran — Beginning in mid-September 2022 after the death in custody of Mahsa Amini, a 22-year-old woman arrested by the morality police for alleged dress-code violations, widespread protests erupted across Iran. Demonstrations quickly spread to dozens of cities and all 31 provinces, driven by demands for justice for Amini, an end to compulsory hijab laws, and broader political and civil reforms. The movement, often referred to as the "Women, Life, Freedom" uprising, involved diverse segments of society, including women, youth, students, and ethnic minority communities and represented one of the most sustained and expansive challenges to the Islamic Republic since 1979. Security forces responded with a severe crackdown, using tear gas, rubber and metal bullets, live ammunition, and mass arrests, resulting in hundreds of confirmed deaths, including minors, and thousands detained according to multiple human rights organizations; the true toll remains disputed due to restrictions on independent reporting and government suppression of information.

consolidate. Live ammunition, mass arrests, communication shutdowns, and aggressive intimidation followed. But unlike previous crackdowns, the ferocity of the response appeared calibrated not only to suppress unrest, but to decapitate what the regime perceived as an emerging political threat.

What distinguished December 2025 was not merely the bloodshed, but the regime's apparent recognition that this uprising was different. For the first time in years, the protests seemed capable of developing both leadership and an alternative political vision. This dual possibility—direction and horizon—was precisely what the Islamic Republic has historically feared most. It is also what led many within the regime to view the December uprising as the most serious challenge to its survival since its founding.

The social composition of the protesters reflected a society shaped by long-term repression and cumulative crisis. A younger generation—many politicized during the Woman, Life, Freedom uprising of 2022—stood alongside workers, unemployed youth, and families devastated by economic collapse. The slogans varied, but they converged on a shared conclusion: trust in the existing political order had completely evaporated. There were no appeals for reform, no calls for legal restoration, and no belief in economic rescue under the current system. The protest was directed at the regime as a whole.

The violent suppression of December 2025 widened an already unbridgeable gap between state and society.[5] For many Iranians, the

---

[5] Nationwide protests in Iran and the December 2025 brutal suppression — Beginning on 28 December 2025, mass demonstrations erupted across Iran in response to deepening economic hardship, rising inflation and the collapse of the Iranian rial, quickly spreading to all 31 provinces and becoming the largest nationwide protest movement since the 1979 Islamic Revolution. Iranian authorities responded with a severe and lethal crackdown that human rights

uprising confirmed what experience had already taught them: the Islamic Republic was neither capable of resolving the crisis nor willing to tolerate an organized alternative. The silence that followed—the denial of casualties, the criminalization of dissent, the threats issued afterward—did not close the chapter. It added another layer to a growing collective memory of state violence, layered atop November 2019 and 2022.

The importance of December 2025 lies not only in what happened, but in what it revealed. Years of relentless repression had failed to produce submission or silence. On the contrary, each crackdown had pushed dissent toward new forms. What made December different was the regime's perception that this wave, unlike many before it, could develop both a political "head" and a vision of what comes after. That perception shaped the brutality of the response—and underscored the depth of the regime's insecurity.

December 2025 was not the beginning of this story. It was the latest and clearest manifestation of a process decades in the making. Each suppressed movement had prepared the ground for the next. This uprising revealed a system that could no longer even simulate

---

organizations, the UN Human Rights Council and international parliaments condemned as "brutal repression" and mass killing of demonstrators. Forces loyal to the Islamic Republic used live ammunition, heavy weapons and mass arrests against largely peaceful crowds, imposed a near-total internet and communications blackout from early January to obscure the scale of violence, and detained tens of thousands of people. Death toll estimates vary amid restricted access to independent verification: Iranian government figures acknowledged thousands killed, while independent sources, including civil society estimates and international reporting, cite several thousand to tens of thousands of deaths and hundreds of thousands of injuries in the first weeks of the uprising. The UN Human Rights Council adopted a resolution urging urgent investigation into serious human rights violations and abuses, including unlawful killings, arbitrary detention, enforced disappearances and torture in connection with these protests.

stability through force alone. Protest returned—heavier with memory, sharper in intent, and more dangerous to contain.

This chapter opens the book because it poses the central question with the greatest urgency: how did a system that survived for decades through repression arrive at a point where society not only rejects it, but begins to imagine a future beyond it? The answer lies not in a single event, but in the path the Islamic Republic has taken over the past twenty-five years—a path in which suppressing social movements did not eliminate dissent, but reproduced it in increasingly destabilizing forms.

The chapters that follow trace that path backward. From early generational fractures to nationwide uprisings, from electoral hope to street politics, from fear to defiance. December 2025 is the pretext for this inquiry—not as an endpoint, but as the most explicit warning yet in a process that is still unfolding.

Introduction

Why This Uprising Was New—and Why It Was Not

To many observers, the protests of December 2025 appeared sudden—another unexpected eruption in a country long accustomed to unrest. Yet what made this uprising deeply unsettling was not its recurrence, but its character: the speed with which it spread, the diversity of its social base, and the intensity of the state's response. Once again, a familiar question resurfaced with renewed urgency: how could a political system that has relied on repression for decades still be forced into confrontation with its own society—without achieving lasting stability? This book is an attempt to answer that question.

December 2025 was neither an anomaly nor an accident. As it was mentioned in earlier pages, it began with a distinctly economic shock: protests by shopkeepers and traders in Tehran's Grand Bazaar against the collapse of the national currency, soaring inflation, and what many openly described as the economic breakdown of the Islamic Republic. The significance of this starting point cannot be overstated. Historically, the bazaar has functioned as a barometer of economic legitimacy and, at times, a stabilizing pillar of the state. When the market itself moved from accommodation to protest, it signaled not a temporary disruption, but a structural rupture.

From there, unrest spread rapidly to other commercial districts, working-class neighborhoods, provincial cities, and economically marginalized regions. What transformed these scattered protests into a nationwide uprising was not a single policy decision, but a collective realization that economic collapse was no longer reversible within the existing system. The protests expressed a broader understanding: the crisis was not cyclical, and the state no longer possessed either the capacity or the will to correct it.

In this sense, December 2025 followed a familiar trajectory. It stood on the accumulated experiences of the past quarter-century. Iranian society had lived through the student protests of 1999,[6] which exposed the first visible generational rupture. It had experienced the Green Movement of 2009,[7] when electoral legitimacy collapsed. It

---

[6] 1999 student uprising in Iran — In July 1999, widespread student protests erupted after the Iranian judiciary shut down the reformist newspaper Salam, a key voice of the reform movement and supporter of then-President Mohammad Khatami's agenda. What began as a peaceful demonstration at Tehran University quickly turned violent when paramilitary forces and state-affiliated vigilantes attacked student dormitories in the early hours of 9 July, beating students, destroying property, and forcibly removing protesters, while uniformed police largely stood by. The crackdown provoked days of unrest in Tehran and other cities, with hundreds wounded, thousands detained, and multiple fatalities—including the acknowledged killing of Ezzat Ebrahim-Nejad and contested reports of further deaths. The 1999 uprising marked a defining moment for Iran's civil society, revealing deep rifts between reformist aspirations and authoritarian resistance and laying early groundwork for later protest movements and demands for political liberalization.

[7] Green Movement (Iran, 2009–2010) — The Iranian Green Movement (*Jonbesh-e Sabz*) arose after the widely disputed 12 June 2009 presidential election, in which incumbent Mahmoud Ahmadinejad was declared the winner amid massive allegations of electoral fraud. Millions of Iranians took to the streets in Tehran and other cities—initially chanting "Where is my vote?" and demanding a recount and respect for constitutional rights—wearing green, the campaign color of reformist candidate Mir-Hossein Mousavi, and calling for political reform and greater civil liberties. The demonstrations represented one of the largest expressions of popular dissent since the 1979 Revolution and embodied long-held aspirations for

had witnessed the entry of marginalized and working-class communities into politics in 2017.[8] It had endured the state's open deployment of mass lethal violence in November 2019. And in 2022, during the Woman, Life, Freedom uprising, it had crossed a psychological threshold by openly rejecting the regime's ideological authority. December 2025 carried the imprint of all these moments. And yet, something crucial had changed.

For the first time in years, a large segment of the protest movement encountered not only a shared rejection of the status quo, but a visible political reference point for what might come next. The public call by Prince Reza Pahlavi—who in recent years had emerged as one of the most recognizable symbols of opposition—played a decisive role in altering the uprising's trajectory. His intervention did not initiate the protests, but it helped elevate them.

---

democratic change in Iranian society. Security forces responded with force, resulting in dozens killed, thousands arrested, brutal crackdowns on protests, and severe restrictions on communications and media. The movement's protest slogan and symbolism persisted in later civic discourse, even as its organizational structure weakened and its leaders—such as Mousavi and Mehdi Karroubi—were placed under house arrest. Although ultimately suppressed by the state, the Green Movement remains a significant chapter in Iran's contemporary struggle over electoral legitimacy and civil rights.

[8] 2017 nationwide protests in Iran (also called the 2017–2018 Iranian protests or *Dey* Protests) — In late December 2017, spontaneous demonstrations broke out in Mashhad and other cities, driven primarily by economic grievances such as rising food prices, unemployment, and dissatisfaction with government mismanagement. These protests rapidly spread to tens of urban centers across Iran, including Tehran, as protesters voiced frustration not only over economic hardship but also over corruption and lack of political reform. The movement was largely leaderless and disorganized, differing from earlier reform-era mobilizations, and reflected deepening public discontent with theocratic governance and elite privilege. Security forces responded with violent crackdowns, resulting in dozens of reported deaths and hundreds to thousands of arrests as tensions escalated and some clashes turned destructive. The protests marked the most intense nationwide challenge to the Islamic Republic since the 2009 Green Movement and foreshadowed later waves of unrest, illustrating enduring socio-economic and political pressures within Iranian society.

It provided many protesters with something that had been conspicuously absent from earlier waves: a sense of leadership and a provisional political horizon.

This distinction mattered profoundly. Previous uprisings were unified primarily by negation—by what protesters opposed. In December 2025, for the first time in a long while, a significant portion of society could articulate not only what it rejected, but also glimpse an alternative future, however incomplete or contested that vision remained. The movement appeared, at least momentarily, capable of developing both a political "head" and a sense of direction. It was precisely this possibility that shaped the regime's response.

The violence unleashed in December 2025 exceeded even the benchmarks set in earlier crackdowns. The state moved with extraordinary speed and brutality to suppress the uprising before it could consolidate. Live ammunition, mass arrests, communication shutdowns, and widespread intimidation followed. This reaction was not merely reflexive. It reflected the regime's assessment that this wave of protest—unlike many before it—posed an existential threat. Not because it was larger, but because it appeared capable of evolving into a movement with leadership and an alternative vision.

The central argument of this book is that the Islamic Republic has moved closer to collapse not despite its repeated repression of social movements, but because of it. Repression is not a neutral or temporary instrument. It destroys political, social, and moral capital. It may buy time in the short term, but it consumes the future. December 2025 revealed how advanced this process had become— how even the simulation of stability now required extreme and immediate violence.

This book does not seek to predict the precise moment of the regime's fall. Collapse here is not understood as a sudden event, but as an accumulative process. Each suppressed movement has weakened the state's capacity to govern, communicate, and legitimate itself. What has changed over time is not only the form of protest, but society's understanding of politics itself—of participation, risk, and possibility. December 2025 was not the end of this trajectory, but one of its clearest manifestations.

The focus on social movements is deliberate. In authoritarian systems, movements expose realities that official institutions conceal. Elections can be engineered, statistics manipulated, and media silenced. But the repeated return of society to the streets—under changing slogans, actors, and risks—cannot be dismissed as coincidence or foreign interference. December 2025 underscored that the crisis confronting the Islamic Republic is not the result of a single policy failure, but the outcome of a long historical path.

Methodologically, this book examines each movement within its political, social, and economic context—not as an isolated eruption, but as part of a continuum. The aim is to identify a pattern: how repression, as the dominant response, produced cumulative consequences that undermined the very system it was meant to preserve. Implicitly, each chapter asks the same question: what did this act of repression destroy for the regime's future?

While informed by lived experience, this is not a memoir. The events of December 2025 serve not as a conclusion, but as a point of entry. From that moment, the narrative moves backward to trace how such an uprising became possible—and why it is unlikely to be the last.

This book is written for readers who want to look beyond breaking news. For those asking why the Islamic Republic, despite its vast coercive apparatus, appears more fragile today than at any previous point in its history. December 2025 posed the question. The chapters that follow attempt to answer it.

Chapter 1

The Post-War Islamic Republic: The Rise of a Security–Economic Order

The Islamic Republic, as it exists today, was not fully formed in 1979. Its defining architecture emerged through a series of political eliminations, institutional constructions, and constitutional recalibrations that unfolded primarily during the first decade after the revolution—and were consolidated in the aftermath of the Iran–Iraq War.[9] The war did not merely devastate the country's economy

---

[9] Iran–Iraq War (1980–1988) — A prolonged and devastating military conflict between the Islamic Republic of Iran and the Republic of Iraq that began on 22 September 1980 when Iraqi forces under Saddam Hussein launched a large-scale invasion of Iranian territory, aiming to seize control of *the Shatt al-Arab* waterway, annex oil-rich regions such as Khuzestan, and exploit Iran's post-revolutionary instability. The war, which lasted nearly eight years and ended in August 1988 with a United Nations-brokered ceasefire and restoration of pre-war borders, became one of the deadliest interstate wars of the 20th century. It was marked by trench warfare, missile and air strikes on cities and infrastructure, the extensive use of chemical weapons by Iraqi forces against Iranian troops and civilians, and extraordinarily high human costs: historians estimate hundreds of thousands to over a million casualties including both combatants and civilians. The conflict wrought immense economic and social destruction on both countries without decisive territorial gains for either side, reshaped regional geopolitics, deepened

and infrastructure; it completed a process of power concentration that fundamentally reshaped the state.

In the revolutionary period, political pluralism—however fragile—briefly existed within the system. Diverse forces participated in the early years of the Islamic Republic, from secular nationalists and leftist groups to Islamist factions with competing visions of governance. This plurality was gradually dismantled. Political opponents were eliminated through a combination of repression, exclusion, and targeted violence. The impeachment and removal of the first president, Abolhassan Banisadr,[10] marked a decisive moment in this process, signaling the regime's intolerance for autonomous centers of power.

Throughout the war years, political assassinations, systematic repression, and ideological purification narrowed the field of power. By the late 1980s, the Islamic Republic had effectively neutralized most of its early rivals. What remained was an increasingly consolidated ruling core—centered around Ali Khamenei,[11] Akbar

---

Iran's isolation, and contributed to the entrenchment of hard-line military and political elites in Tehran.

[10] Abolhassan Banisadr — Abolhassan Banisadr (1933–2021) was the first president of the Islamic Republic of Iran, elected in January 1980 in the immediate aftermath of the 1979 Revolution. An economist educated in France and an early ally of Ayatollah Ruhollah Khomeini, Banisadr initially played a central role in shaping the post-revolutionary state. His presidency, however, was marked by escalating conflict with clerical hard-liners, particularly over the concentration of power in unelected institutions and the growing influence of the Islamic Revolutionary Guard Corps. Amid the turmoil of the early years of the Iran–Iraq War, Banisadr was impeached by the Majles in June 1981, accused of incompetence and opposition to clerical authority, and subsequently removed from office. He fled Iran later that year and lived in exile in France, where he remained a persistent critic of the Islamic Republic, arguing that the revolution's republican and democratic promises were undermined by the consolidation of clerical rule.

[11] Ali Khamenei — Ali Khamenei (b. 1939) has served as the Supreme Leader of the Islamic Republic of Iran since 1989, following the death of Ayatollah Ruhollah

Hashemi Rafsanjani,[12] and Ahmad Khomeini[13]—that moved to monopolize authority while preserving the appearance of revolutionary continuity.

Khomeini. Previously, he was president from 1981 to 1989, a period shaped by the latter half of the Iran–Iraq War and the consolidation of post-revolutionary power. As Supreme Leader, Khamenei holds ultimate authority over Iran's political system, commanding the armed forces, appointing the heads of key institutions—including the judiciary, state media, and the Guardian Council—and exercising decisive influence over elected bodies. Over more than three decades, his leadership has been marked by the steady centralization of power, the expansion of security and intelligence institutions, and the systematic suppression of dissent, positioning the office of the Supreme Leader as the core pillar sustaining authoritarian rule within the Islamic Republic.

[12] Akbar Hashemi Rafsanjani — Akbar Hashemi Rafsanjani (1934–2017) was a central figure in the consolidation and evolution of the Islamic Republic, serving as Speaker of Parliament during the Iran–Iraq War, President from 1989 to 1997, and later as Chairman of the Expediency Discernment Council. A close associate of Ayatollah Ruhollah Khomeini, Rafsanjani played a key role in wartime decision-making and in managing Iran's post-war reconstruction. His presidency emphasized economic liberalization, infrastructure development, and limited engagement with the outside world, while leaving the core authoritarian structure of the system intact. In later years, Rafsanjani increasingly positioned himself as a pragmatic critic of hard-line policies, especially after the 2009 Green Movement, though his influence was steadily curtailed by unelected power centers. His political career illustrates the tension between pragmatism and authoritarian consolidation within the Islamic Republic's elite.

[13] Ahmad Khomeini — Ahmad Khomeini (1945–1995) was the younger son of Ayatollah Ruhollah Khomeini and a pivotal behind-the-scenes figure during the first decade of the Islamic Republic. Serving as his father's chief aide and gatekeeper, he controlled access to the Supreme Leader and played an influential role in transmitting decisions, managing correspondence, and mediating among rival revolutionary factions. Ahmad Khomeini was closely associated with key power struggles of the 1980s, including the marginalization of early revolutionary figures and the consolidation of clerical authority during and after the Iran–Iraq War. After Ayatollah Khomeini's death in 1989, his political influence declined rapidly, particularly following the elevation of Ali Khamenei to the position of Supreme Leader. Ahmad Khomeini died under contested circumstances in 1995, and his role remains emblematic of the informal yet decisive power exercised within the inner circles of the post-revolutionary state.

The war provided the conditions necessary for this consolidation. Under the logic of national survival, extraordinary powers were normalized. Security, military, and intelligence institutions expanded rapidly, operating with minimal oversight. The Islamic Revolutionary Guard Corps[14] evolved from a revolutionary militia into a central pillar of power, while parallel institutions— foundations (*bonyads*), security bodies, and informal networks— grew alongside the formal state. These entities operated beyond transparency, blurring the line between governance, coercion, and economic control.

Internal conflicts within the wartime leadership further shaped the post-war order. The political and economic tensions between Ali Khamenei and Prime Minister Mir-Hossein Mousavi[15] during the

---

[14] Islamic Revolutionary Guard Corps (IRGC) — Established in May 1979 in the immediate aftermath of the Iranian Revolution, the Islamic Revolutionary Guard Corps was created to protect the revolutionary order and the authority of the clerical leadership, operating parallel to—and often in competition with—the regular armed forces (*Artesh*). Over time, the IRGC evolved from an ideologically driven paramilitary force into a multifaceted power center, encompassing ground, naval, aerospace, intelligence, and cyber units, as well as the Basij militia, which has played a central role in domestic repression. During the Iran–Iraq War (1980–1988), the IRGC expanded its military and political influence, a trajectory that continued in the post-war period through deep involvement in Iran's economy, media, and regional proxy operations. Today, the IRGC functions not only as a military institution but as a core pillar of authoritarian governance, instrumental in suppressing protests, shaping foreign policy, and safeguarding the survival of the Islamic Republic's ruling structure.

[15] Mir-Hossein Mousavi — Mir-Hossein Mousavi (b. 1942) served as Prime Minister of Iran from 1981 to 1989, during the most intense years of the Iran–Iraq War, overseeing a state-controlled wartime economy and playing a central role in crisis governance. After the post was abolished in the 1989 constitutional revisions, he largely withdrew from frontline politics until reemerging as a leading reformist candidate in the 2009 presidential election. Following the disputed election results, Mousavi became the principal figurehead of the Green Movement, articulating demands for electoral integrity, civil rights, and constitutional accountability. The state's response to the movement led to his house arrest in February 2011, where he has remained without formal charges or trial. Mousavi's

war years reflected competing visions of state management and redistribution. These conflicts did not disappear with the end of the war; they were resolved through structural change rather than compromise. The sidelining of Ayatollah Hossein Ali Montazeri[16]— once designated as the successor to Ruhollah Khomeini—removed a key internal critic of unchecked repression and cleared the path for a more centralized and disciplined power structure.

This consolidation reached its institutional culmination in the post-war constitutional amendments of 1989.[17] Changes to the

---

political trajectory—from revolutionary insider to symbol of dissent—reflects the narrowing space for reform and the consolidation of authoritarian power within the Islamic Republic.

[16] Hossein Ali Montazeri — Ayatollah Hossein Ali Montazeri (1922–2009) was one of the most senior clerics of the Islamic Republic and originally designated as Ayatollah Ruhollah Khomeini's successor in the 1980s. A leading architect of the post-revolutionary constitutional order and an early proponent of *velayat-e faqih*, Montazeri later became its most prominent internal critic. His open opposition to widespread human rights abuses—most notably his condemnation of the 1988 mass executions of political prisoners—led to his political marginalization and removal as heir apparent in 1989. Placed under years of house arrest, Montazeri continued to argue that unchecked clerical power violated both Islamic ethics and popular sovereignty. In his final years, he emerged as a moral reference point for reformists and dissidents, openly supporting protest movements and calling for limits on the authority of the Supreme Leader. His legacy embodies the unresolved tension between religious authority and accountability within the Islamic Republic.

[17] 1989 constitutional amendments in Iran — In July 1989, shortly after the death of Ayatollah Ruhollah Khomeini, the Islamic Republic adopted a set of constitutional amendments through a national referendum that fundamentally reshaped the political structure of the state. The revisions abolished the office of prime minister, concentrating executive authority in the presidency; expanded the powers of the Supreme Leader, including formal control over the armed forces and key appointments; and removed the requirement that the Supreme Leader be a *marja'-e taqlid*, thereby enabling the elevation of Ali Khamenei to the position despite his lower clerical rank. The amendments also strengthened the role of unelected bodies such as the Expediency Discernment Council, institutionalizing mechanisms to override parliamentary decisions. Collectively, these changes marked a decisive shift away from the republic's early, more pluralistic framework

constitution significantly strengthened the position of the Supreme Leader while weakening mechanisms of accountability and balance. These revisions did not merely adjust the political system; they entrenched authoritarianism by design. Power was no longer contested within the revolutionary framework—it was structurally secured in the hands of a narrow ruling group.

When the war ended in 1988, the regime confronted a new challenge. Revolutionary mobilization had lost its force, and the external threat that justified emergency governance had receded. The question facing the leadership was no longer how to defend the revolution militarily, but how to preserve power in a society exhausted by war and increasingly disconnected from revolutionary ideology. The answer was not political opening, but the securitization of governance.

From Revolutionary Emergency to Permanent Security

Post-war reconstruction did not lead to a renegotiation of the social contract. Instead, it marked the transition from revolutionary emergency to permanent security. Institutions that had expanded during the war—most notably the Revolutionary Guards and intelligence bodies—were no longer confined to military or defensive roles. They became instruments of internal order and guarantors of regime survival.

Security ceased to be an exceptional condition. It became the organizing principle of governance. Political dissent, social critique, labor activism, and cultural expression were increasingly framed as threats to national stability. By the mid-1990s, the Islamic Republic

---

toward a more centralized and personalized system of clerical rule, with long-term consequences for political accountability and the balance of power in Iran.

had begun to redefine politics itself—not as a space of participation, but as a domain to be managed, monitored, and contained.

The Economy as a Mechanism of Control

Economic reconstruction after the war unfolded within this security framework. Rather than rebuilding inclusive institutions capable of distributing opportunity broadly, the state developed an economy in which access to resources was closely tied to political loyalty. A vast network of semi-opaque enterprises emerged, many linked directly or indirectly to security and military institutions.

The Revolutionary Guards, in particular, transitioned into a dominant economic actor, securing major contracts in construction, energy, telecommunications, and infrastructure. Economic power and coercive capacity became mutually reinforcing. This arrangement created a class of stakeholders whose material interests were bound to the survival of the system, while marginalizing those excluded from these networks.

Inequality widened, but it was not accidental. It was structured. Those connected to power advanced, while large segments of society—especially in provincial and working-class areas—were left behind. Economic grievance became embedded in political exclusion.

Hollowed-Out Politics and the Illusion of Participation

As the security–economic order solidified, politics was gradually emptied of substantive choice. Elections continued, parties existed in name, and representative institutions remained formally intact.

Yet real decision-making increasingly shifted to unelected bodies operating beyond public accountability.

This separation between appearance and power produced a profound sense of alienation. Participation persisted as ritual, but its meaning eroded. For younger generations in particular, politics felt performative—something staged rather than lived, managed rather than contested.

During the 1990s, these contradictions remained largely latent. Post-war legitimacy, limited economic recovery, and the absence of large-scale unrest allowed the regime to maintain surface stability. But beneath that stability, social and generational fractures were deepening.

Universities as Early Warning Sites

Universities were among the first spaces where these tensions became visible. Expanded access to higher education produced a generation shaped not by revolutionary experience, but by post-war realities. These students were more urban, more globally connected, and more attuned to the gap between official narratives and lived conditions.

For them, the promises of reconstruction rang hollow. Education no longer guaranteed mobility, political participation was tightly constrained, and cultural life was heavily policed. Universities thus became early warning sites—spaces where the contradictions of the post-war order surfaced before reaching the broader society.

The state's response was containment. Surveillance intensified, student organizations were restricted, and critical voices were disciplined. What emerged was a model of preemptive repression—intervening before dissent could spread beyond controlled environments.

Closing the Channels of Release

This strategy carried a hidden cost. By restricting legal and institutional channels for expressing dissatisfaction, the state narrowed the avenues through which social pressure could be released. Grievances did not disappear; they accumulated.

The post-war Islamic Republic chose stability through control rather than adaptability through reform. In the short term, this choice appeared effective. The system endured, economic growth resumed unevenly, and overt unrest remained limited. But beneath the surface, a generational disconnect was taking shape—one that would soon find its first mass expression.

This chapter marked the true starting point of the trajectory traced in this book. A regime that emerged from war committed to managing society through security and exclusion laid the groundwork for a recurring cycle: social mobilization followed by repression, each round more costly than the last. The first visible rupture in this cycle would appear at the end of the decade, when university campuses became the epicenter of a challenge the state believed it had already neutralized.

The next chapter turns to that moment—the student uprising of 1999—and examines how the first major post-war protest exposed the limits of control and inaugurated a much longer confrontation between society and the state.

Chapter 2

The 1999 Student Uprising: The First Visible Generational Rupture

The student uprising of July 1999 did not emerge in a political vacuum. It unfolded in the immediate aftermath of one of the most hopeful moments in the history of the Islamic Republic: the presidential election of May 1997.[18] That election, which brought Mohammad Khatami[19] to power, had generated unprecedented

---

[18] 1997 presidential election in Iran — Held on 23 May 1997, the seventh presidential election marked a pivotal turning point in the post-revolutionary political landscape. In a landslide victory, Mohammad Khatami, a relatively little-known cleric and former minister of culture, defeated establishment-backed candidates with nearly 70 percent of the vote, propelled by exceptionally high voter turnout. His campaign resonated strongly with youth, women, students, and the urban middle class, emphasizing the rule of law, civil society, political freedoms, and a "dialogue of civilizations" in foreign policy. The election exposed a deep gap between society and entrenched power centers and signaled popular demand for reform within the framework of the Islamic Republic. While Khatami's presidency raised widespread hopes for gradual democratization, it also triggered sustained resistance from unelected institutions, foreshadowing the structural limits that would later constrain reformist politics in Iran.

[19] Mohammad Khatami — Mohammad Khatami (b. 1943) served as President of Iran from 1997 to 2005, emerging as the leading figure of the country's post-revolutionary reform movement after his landslide victory in the 1997 election. A cleric and former minister of culture, Khatami campaigned on promises of the rule of law, civil society, freedom of expression, and political participation, galvanizing broad support among youth, women, students, and the urban middle class. His presidency fostered a brief opening in Iran's political and cultural space,

expectations among large segments of Iranian society—particularly students, intellectuals, and urban youth—that meaningful change might finally be possible through legal and institutional means.

The reformist current that won the election presented a clear promise. By capturing elected institutions through the ballot box, it argued, reformers could gradually reinterpret the constitution, expand civil liberties, strengthen the role of representative bodies, and reduce the dominance of unelected power centers. The message was explicit: change would not come through confrontation, but through participation; not through rupture, but through reform from within.

For a time, this promise appeared plausible. The post-1997 period witnessed limited but visible openings. The number of newspapers and journals increased. Civil society organizations became more active. Public debate, especially on university campuses, grew more vibrant. These developments were modest and fragile, but they were enough to convince many that the system might be capable of self-correction. It was precisely this context that made the events of July 1999 so consequential.

What began as a protest against the closure of a reformist newspaper quickly escalated into a broader confrontation. On the surface, the trigger seemed procedural: a press ban, student demonstrations, and a security response. Yet the ferocity of that

---

marked by a flourishing of independent media and public debate, as well as an outward-looking foreign policy framed around his concept of a "Dialogue of Civilizations." However, sustained resistance from unelected institutions—particularly the judiciary, security forces, and the Guardian Council—severely constrained his reform agenda. Khatami's tenure ultimately highlighted both the popular demand for change and the structural barriers to meaningful reform within the Islamic Republic's power system.

response—particularly the violent attack on student dormitories at Tehran University—revealed that the issue was far deeper than media regulation.

The crackdown exposed a fundamental contradiction at the heart of the reformist project. While elected institutions existed, they did not control the instruments of coercion. The security forces, intelligence bodies, and vigilante groups that stormed the dormitories operated beyond the reach of the very institutions that had promised reform. When violence was followed by selective prosecutions that punished protesters rather than perpetrators, the limits of electoral power became unmistakable. This was not merely a political setback. It was a formative experience.

For the generation that had placed its hopes in the ballot box, July 1999 marked the first direct encounter with the structural boundaries of reform. The belief that gradual, legal change was possible within the existing framework suffered its first serious blow—not as an abstract theoretical realization, but as lived reality. The system revealed itself as one in which elections could alter tone and rhetoric, but not the distribution of power.

Socially, the uprising was distinctly generational. Its participants were overwhelmingly students—young, urban, and educated— many of whom had grown up after the revolution and felt little attachment to its founding narratives. Their demands were not revolutionary in the classical sense. They did not call for the overthrow of the Islamic Republic. Instead, they demanded accountability, dignity, and the fulfillment of the promises implied by constitutional governance.

Their language reflected this orientation. Slogans appealed to law, rights, and popular sovereignty rather than ideology. This framing gave the movement moral force, but also limited its reach. While it resonated deeply within universities and among the urban middle class, it struggled to mobilize broader social groups whose grievances were more immediately economic.

This limitation made suppression easier. The state was able to isolate the uprising, portray it as elitist, and crush it without triggering nationwide unrest. Yet the political consequences of suppression extended far beyond the campuses.

The uprising unfolded against a backdrop of growing economic insecurity. Post-war reconstruction had failed to deliver equitable opportunity, and for many students, higher education no longer guaranteed employment or social mobility. Patronage networks and political loyalty increasingly determined access to resources. The gap between expectation and reality widened, intensifying the sense of betrayal felt by a generation that had invested in institutional participation.

The state's response to the uprising established a pattern that would be repeated for decades. Rather than addressing underlying grievances, authorities chose containment. Student organizations were dismantled, activists imprisoned, and campuses subjected to heightened surveillance. What emerged was a model of preemptive repression—aimed not only at suppressing dissent, but at preventing its reappearance.

In the short term, this strategy succeeded. Order was restored, visible protest subsided, and the reformist project continued in a weakened and constrained form. But the cost was substantial.

Universities were transformed from sites of managed critique into reservoirs of latent opposition. The lesson absorbed by many students was clear: even limited, system-loyal demands could provoke violence if they crossed invisible red lines.

The 1999 student uprising did not overthrow the regime, nor did it immediately transform Iran's political structure. Its significance lies in what it revealed and what it destroyed. It marked the first moment when a large segment of society directly experienced the futility of relying solely on legal and electoral pathways for change.

For the state, suppressing the uprising appeared to reaffirm control. For society, it planted the seeds of long-term distrust. That distrust would resurface in later crises, shaping how Iranians interpreted promises, elections, and calls for patience. When millions returned to the streets a decade later to contest the results of another election, they did so with the memory of 1999 already embedded in their political consciousness. Peaceful protest, they knew, offered no guarantees of protection. Reform, they understood, had limits imposed from above.

The student uprising of 1999 thus stands as the opening rupture in a much longer cycle. It revealed the early incompatibility between a changing society and a rigid political structure—and demonstrated how repression, even when effective in the short term, could generate deeper and more consequential challenges in the years ahead.

The next chapter turns to the Green Movement of 2009, when the lessons of 1999 were replayed on a national scale, transforming electoral disappointment into a full-blown crisis of political legitimacy.

Chapter 3

The Green Movement of 2009: The Collapse of Electoral Legitimacy

The Green Movement of 2009 marked a decisive rupture in the political life of the Islamic Republic—not simply because of its scale, but because it fundamentally altered how political change was imagined and pursued. For the first time since the establishment of the regime, the ballot box ceased to function as the uncontested horizon of reformist politics, and the street emerged—openly and unmistakably—as a legitimate arena of political demand. This transformation was as significant for who led it as for how it unfolded.

Unlike earlier protests, the Green Movement was initiated and endorsed by political forces that had long insisted on strict adherence to electoral mechanisms. For years, reformist leaders had discouraged street mobilization, framing it as dangerous, destabilizing, or counterproductive. Popular participation was encouraged primarily at election time, through controlled and institutional channels. In 2009, that logic broke down.

Beyond the Ballot Box

The disputed presidential election of June 2009 unfolded amid extraordinary political engagement. Voter turnout was high, public debates were unusually energetic, and expectations of change were widespread—particularly after four years of Mahmoud Ahmadinejad's confrontational governance, economic mismanagement, and international isolation. For many Iranians, the election appeared to offer a genuine opportunity to redirect the country's course through lawful means.

The Green Movement began with a modest and system-loyal demand: Where is my vote? Protesters did not initially reject the Islamic Republic or its constitutional framework. They appealed to the regime's own claims—fair elections, popular sovereignty, and legal accountability. In doing so, they placed the system on trial by its own standards.

Yet when the state responded not with transparency but with force, the meaning of the protest shifted. The rapid announcement of results widely perceived as implausible, followed by the refusal to conduct a credible review, transformed an electoral dispute into a legitimacy crisis. The message was unmistakable: elections existed, but their outcomes were not negotiable.

At that moment, the movement crossed a threshold. The street— once treated by reformists as a last resort—became unavoidable. Demonstrations were no longer supplementary to the ballot box; they were its extension. For the first time, political actors who had previously confined dissent to institutional channels openly embraced mass street mobilization as a tool of pressure.

33

The Street as Political Actor

This was a qualitative shift in Iran's post-revolutionary politics. The Green Movement did not abandon electoral legitimacy—it attempted to defend it by mobilizing society beyond the ballot box. In doing so, it implicitly acknowledged what earlier reformist discourse had denied: that controlled institutions alone were insufficient to compel change.

The scale of participation was unprecedented. Millions of citizens—students, professionals, artists, civil servants, and even former insiders—filled the streets of major cities. Digital networks facilitated rapid coordination, while shared symbols and slogans created a sense of national unity. For a brief moment, the movement appeared capable of forcing accountability without rejecting the system outright. It was precisely this possibility that triggered the regime's response.

Repression as a Turning Point

The suppression of the Green Movement was swift, systematic, and transformative. Peaceful demonstrations were met with violence. Protest leaders were arrested or placed under house arrest. Public spaces were militarized, media silenced, and dissent reframed as foreign-backed subversion. The state did not merely disperse crowds; it sought to delegitimize protest itself.

This repression marked one of the most consequential turning points in the Islamic Republic's history. A movement that had begun by demanding recognition of votes was answered with batons, bullets, and prisons. In that exchange, the credibility of the ballot box suffered a blow from which it would not recover.

What collapsed in 2009 was not only a protest movement, but a political belief: that elections, even when mobilizing millions, could serve as reliable instruments of structural change under authoritarian constraints.

A Broad Coalition—and Its Limits

Socially, the Green Movement was broader than any protest since the revolution. It united diverse segments of society under a shared demand for political accountability. Yet this breadth was uneven. The movement drew its strength primarily from urban middle classes and educated constituencies. Large parts of the working class and rural populations—already skeptical of electoral politics or temporarily benefiting from populist redistribution—remained largely outside its orbit.

This limitation proved consequential. It allowed the state to isolate the movement socially and frame it as elitist. While this narrative was deeply misleading, it was effective enough to prevent the formation of a truly cross-class coalition capable of sustaining resistance under repression.

The End of Electoral Illusions

The aftermath of 2009 reshaped Iranian political consciousness. Elections continued to be held, but their meaning changed. Participation increasingly appeared as ritual rather than agency, management rather than choice. For many citizens, the lesson was devastatingly clear: even mass participation and peaceful protest could be met with uncompromising violence.

Political energy did not disappear—it migrated. Some withdrew into apathy or private life. Others radicalized. Over time, dissent shifted away from institutional reform toward more confrontational and survival-driven forms of protest.

For the state, the suppression of the Green Movement secured short-term control. For society, it marked the collapse of faith in the ballot box as a pathway to change. The regime preserved elections, but forfeited their legitimacy.

A Reconfigured Landscape

In retrospect, the Green Movement represents the moment when the Islamic Republic lost its monopoly over the meaning of political legitimacy. The state continued to invoke elections as proof of consent, but a growing segment of society no longer accepted that claim.

The consequences of this rupture would unfold over the following decade. When protests erupted in 2017 and beyond, they did so without appeals to electoral justice or reformist promises. The language of politics shifted—from votes to livelihoods, from legality to dignity, from participation to resistance.

The Green Movement did not overthrow the system. But it transformed the relationship between citizens and power. It revealed the limits of reformism under authoritarian rule and demonstrated how repression, when deployed against peaceful mass mobilization, can destroy not only movements—but the mechanisms that once sustained political belief.

The next chapter turns to the protests of 2017, when electoral disillusionment converged with economic desperation, and a new set of actors entered the streets—no longer asking where their vote was, but whether the system itself had anything left to offer.

Chapter 4

The 2017 Protests: The Entry of the Marginalized and the End of Reform from Below

The protests that erupted across Iran in late December 2017 marked a decisive shift in the country's trajectory of dissent. They did not arise from electoral controversy or demands for political reform, but from deepening economic despair. More importantly, they emerged after the collapse of two successive strategies for change: reform through the ballot box and economic relief through international engagement.

In the aftermath of the violent suppression of the Green Movement in 2009, the political landscape was reshaped through tightly controlled elections that produced a government promising moderation rather than reform. The central message of this new political moment was pragmatic rather than transformative. The state would not open politically, but it would seek economic relief by reducing international isolation, negotiating over the nuclear file, and easing sanctions. This strategy culminated in the election of Hassan Rouhani in 2013.[20]

For a brief period, this approach appeared to work. The nuclear agreement generated cautious optimism. Sanctions relief brought limited international reengagement, modest economic growth, and renewed expectations that daily life might improve. For many Iranians—particularly those exhausted by years of political repression—the promise of economic stabilization without political confrontation seemed acceptable, even preferable. Change, once again, appeared possible without challenging the core of power.

Yet this opening was shallow and tightly constrained. From the outset, the Islamic Republic's supreme authority viewed international engagement not as an opportunity for transformation, but as a threat. Ali Khamenei repeatedly framed the nuclear agreement as a potential gateway for Western influence, cultural penetration, and political destabilization. As a result, the economic benefits of the deal were deliberately limited. Structural reforms were blocked, investment was constrained, and key sectors of the economy remained under the control of security-linked institutions.

---

[20] 2013 Iranian presidential election and Hassan Rouhani — The 11th presidential election in Iran was held on 14 June 2013 to choose a successor to outgoing Mahmoud Ahmadinejad, who was ineligible to run due to constitutional term limits. After the Guardian Council vetted hundreds of registrants and approved only a small slate of candidates, Hassan Rouhani, a cleric with a reputation as a pragmatist and moderate, secured just over 50 percent of the vote—enough to win outright in the first round without a runoff. His campaign was backed by reformists and moderates seeking a shift from hard-line policies, and the high turnout of about 73 percent was widely interpreted as a popular desire for change in both domestic policy and international engagement. Rouhani's victory was seen domestically and internationally as a mandate for a more conciliatory approach, particularly on economic issues and Iran's nuclear program, though his ability to implement reforms remained constrained by the Islamic Republic's powerful unelected institutions.

The message was clear: negotiations could ease pressure, but they would not alter the framework of governance.

As a result, the economic relief experienced after the agreement was uneven and fragile. Inflation returned, unemployment remained high, and inequality deepened. The benefits of limited international opening accrued primarily to those already connected to power, while large segments of society—particularly in provincial towns and marginalized regions—saw little improvement. For them, the promise of economic normalization proved as illusory as earlier promises of political reform. It was within this context of compounded disappointment that the protests of 2017 erupted.

From Disillusionment to Economic Revolt

By late 2017, trust in both political and economic pathways to change had largely evaporated. Elections had failed to produce reform. Negotiations had failed to deliver material security. What remained was a society confronting rising prices, unpaid wages, collapsing local economies, and the visible enrichment of a narrow elite.

The protests that emerged reflected this reality. Demonstrators did not invoke constitutional rights or electoral slogans. They spoke instead in the language of survival: unemployment, inflation, corruption, and inequality. Yet even as the protests began with economic demands, they quickly took on a political character. Slogans expanded beyond material grievances to target the system itself, signaling that economic suffering was no longer understood as a policy failure, but as a feature of the political order. This shift was critical. It marked the politicization of poverty.

New Actors, New Geography

The social composition of the 2017 protests distinguished them sharply from earlier movements. Participants were overwhelmingly drawn from marginalized groups: unemployed youth, informal workers, retirees, and residents of small towns and peripheral cities long excluded from economic opportunity. These were constituencies often assumed to be politically passive—or even supportive of the system.

Their entry into the streets signaled that dissent had moved beyond the traditional bases of protest. The geographic spread of demonstrations—far from Tehran's political centers—revealed the depth of social fracture and the national scope of economic despair.

The protests were decentralized, spontaneous, and largely leaderless. There were no prominent figures to arrest, no organizations to dismantle, and no reformist elites to negotiate with. This structure made the movement difficult to co-opt, but also limited its ability to sustain momentum.

The Securitization of Economic Grievance

The state's response to the 2017 protests revealed a critical shift in governance. Economic grievances were no longer treated as social problems requiring policy solutions. They were redefined as security threats.

By framing poverty, unemployment, and regional inequality as risks to national stability, the regime narrowed the space for economic debate. Protest was met with arrests, intimidation, and information control rather than redistribution or reform. Economic management was subordinated to order maintenance.

This choice carried long-term consequences. By securitizing poverty, the state acknowledged—implicitly—that it lacked the capacity or willingness to address the structural roots of discontent. Repression replaced reform not only politically, but economically.

The End of Reform from Below

The 2017 protests marked the definitive end of reform from below. They demonstrated that neither electoral participation nor economic patience could secure meaningful change. The language of reform—already weakened after 2009—lost its remaining credibility among the very groups most affected by economic crisis.

Although the protests subsided under pressure, their impact was enduring. The social base of dissent had expanded irreversibly, and the logic of protest had shifted. Opposition no longer depended on reformist leadership or institutional frameworks. It emerged organically from material hardship.

For the regime, the protests were deeply unsettling. They revealed that economic desperation alone could mobilize society—and that repression was the only remaining response.

The suppression of the 2017 protests closed yet another channel for peaceful expression. By refusing both political reform and economic restructuring, the state set the stage for a far more violent confrontation. When the next shock arrived—an abrupt fuel price increase in November 2019—the accumulated frustrations of marginalized communities would erupt with unprecedented intensity.

The next chapter examines that rupture. November 2019 marked the moment when the Islamic Republic abandoned even the pretense of restraint, deploying mass lethal violence to contain a protest born of economic collapse. It was a turning point not only in the use of force, but in society's understanding of the true costs of dissent.

Chapter 5

November 2019: Mass Violence and the Point of No Return

The protests of November 2019 marked a watershed moment in the relationship between the Islamic Republic and Iranian society. If the protests of 2017 had revealed the politicization of economic despair, November 2019 exposed something far more consequential: the regime's readiness to deploy mass lethal violence against its own population as a routine instrument of control. This was not simply another episode of repression. It was the moment when violence ceased to be exceptional and became openly constitutive of governance.

The immediate trigger was the abrupt and overnight increase in fuel prices—a decision announced without warning, consultation, or mitigation. The move came amid severe economic strain. Inflation was accelerating, unemployment remained high, and the renewed impact of international sanctions was being felt most acutely by low-income households. For millions of Iranians, the fuel hike was not an isolated policy choice; it was the final confirmation of a governing logic that imposed hardship from above while insulating centers of power from consequence.

As in earlier uprisings, the policy itself was not the cause so much as the catalyst. What erupted in November 2019 was the accumulated anger of communities already pushed to the margins by years of economic exclusion and political abandonment. Protests spread rapidly across dozens of cities, particularly in provincial and working-class areas. Their speed and geographic breadth signaled a level of nationwide discontent that could no longer be dismissed as localized unrest or elite agitation.

A Preemptive Strategy of Force

The regime's response was immediate, coordinated, and uncompromising. Within hours, security forces moved to suppress demonstrations using overwhelming force. Live ammunition was deployed extensively. Hundreds were killed within days. Simultaneously, the state imposed a near-total nationwide internet shutdown—one of the most extensive information blackouts in the country's history—severing communication among protesters and isolating the violence from public scrutiny.

This response was neither improvised nor reactive. It reflected a preemptive strategy aimed at preventing the protests from evolving into a sustained movement. The objective was not to restore order gradually, but to crush dissent decisively before it could acquire momentum, leadership, or narrative coherence.

What distinguished November 2019 from earlier crackdowns was not only the scale of violence, but the absence of restraint. In previous confrontations, repression had often been accompanied by legal pretexts, selective enforcement, or rhetorical appeals to national security. In November 2019, violence itself became the message. The state demonstrated that it was willing to incur domestic trauma and international condemnation to preserve control.

The Social Geography of Repression

The burden of violence fell disproportionately on marginalized communities. Many of the highest casualty counts were reported in poorer neighborhoods and peripheral cities—areas that had already borne the heaviest economic costs of sanctions, mismanagement, and inequality. This pattern reinforced a grim social truth: certain segments of society were treated as expendable.

The protests themselves were decentralized and largely leaderless, reflecting the erosion of organized political structures capable of mediating dissent. There were no prominent figures to negotiate with, no reformist elites to pressure, and no institutional channels left to absorb social anger. The state responded accordingly—not by dialogue or concession, but by treating the protests as a security threat to be eliminated.

The Collapse of Moral Legitimacy

The aftermath of November 2019 was marked by denial and silence. Official narratives minimized the scale of the killings, refused to release casualty figures, and framed the unrest as foreign-instigated sabotage. Families of victims were harassed and threatened. Public mourning was suppressed.

For many Iranians, this response represented a moral breaking point. The mass killing of unarmed protesters, followed by systematic denial, shattered any remaining belief that the state recognized moral or political accountability toward its citizens.

Control was maintained, but legitimacy suffered a profound and irreversible blow.

Fear returned to the streets—but it was a transformed fear. It was no longer shaped by uncertainty about how far the state might go. That question had been answered. Society now understood the true cost of dissent and the regime's willingness to pay it. This knowledge did not extinguish opposition; it recalibrated it.

Violence as a Governing Principle

November 2019 revealed the extent to which violence had become embedded in the Islamic Republic's mode of rule. Repression was no longer a last resort or crisis response. It was a governing principle—one that narrowed the regime's future options. Having demonstrated its readiness to kill on a mass scale, the state forfeited the ability to credibly present itself as a reformer, mediator, or protector of public welfare.

At the same time, reliance on extreme force carried its own risks. Each act of repression deepened alienation, intensified grievance, and made future confrontations more volatile. The protests were suppressed, but the underlying crisis was sharpened rather than resolved.

A Threshold Crossed

In retrospect, November 2019 stands as a point of no return. It did not end protest in Iran, but it fundamentally altered its trajectory. Subsequent movements would emerge with far fewer illusions and a clearer understanding of the nature of the state they confronted.

The memory of November 2019 became a reference point for everything that followed. It shaped how society interpreted state behavior and calibrated risk. When Iranians returned to the streets in 2022 under the banner of Woman, Life, Freedom, they did so in the shadow of this experience—aware that the regime had already crossed a line it would not retreat from.

The next chapter turns to that uprising. Unlike earlier protests driven primarily by economic grievance or electoral dispute, the movement of 2022 confronted the ideological foundations of the system itself. It challenged not only how the Islamic Republic governed, but why it claimed the right to govern at all.

Chapter 6

Woman, Life, Freedom (2022): Revolt Against the Ideological Order

The uprising that swept across Iran in the fall of 2022 marked a profound transformation in the nature of dissent. If November 2019 had exposed the regime's readiness to kill in order to rule, 2022 revealed something equally consequential: a society willing to confront the system despite full awareness of that violence. This was not a protest rooted in electoral dispute or economic policy. It was a revolt against the ideological foundations of the Islamic Republic itself. What was at stake was no longer a specific demand or grievance, but the regime's claim to regulate identity, morality, and everyday life.

The immediate trigger was the death of Mahsa Amini while in the custody of Iran's morality police. Yet the speed, scale, and persistence of the protests made clear that the outrage far exceeded a single case. Amini's death crystallized years of accumulated humiliation, gendered coercion, and everyday violence—particularly directed at women—and transformed them into a

49

nationwide uprising. What had long been normalized as social control was suddenly exposed as systemic domination.

In this sense, 2022 did not emerge in isolation. It unfolded in the long shadow of November 2019. Society had already learned how far the state was willing to go. What changed was not the level of repression, but the meaning attached to it.

Beyond Reform, Beyond Survival

From its earliest moments, the Woman, Life, Freedom uprising defied familiar political categories. It did not seek reform through institutions that had already been hollowed out. Nor did it organize around electoral promises or elite negotiations. Instead, it articulated a fundamental rejection of the regime's moral authority—the belief that the state possessed the right to dictate how people should dress, behave, love, or exist in public space.

This marked a decisive break with earlier protest cycles. In 2017 and 2019, economic survival had been the dominant frame. In 2022, the struggle was existential. The protest was not about improving conditions within the system, but about contesting the system's right to impose meaning and control.

The centrality of women was not symbolic; it was structural. Women were not merely participants in the uprising—they were its protagonists. Acts of defiance such as removing headscarves, cutting hair in public, and openly confronting morality police became political acts of the highest order. In a system where control over women's bodies had long functioned as a cornerstone of ideological authority, these gestures struck at the heart of the regime's self-definition.

A Generational Threshold

Socially, the uprising was driven by a generation shaped by cumulative disillusionment. Many participants had no living memory of the revolution, the war, or even the reformist moment of the late 1990s. Their political consciousness had been formed instead by the repeated closure of legal pathways to change, by economic precarity, and by the memory of state violence.

This generation did not speak the language of gradualism or compromise. Its relationship to the state was not defined by disappointment, but by estrangement. The Islamic Republic was no longer perceived as a flawed system in need of reform, but as an alien structure imposed upon society.

Digital culture amplified this rupture. Social media transformed individual acts of defiance into shared symbols, collapsing the distance between private resistance and public protest. Music, art, humor, and satire became tools of political expression, undermining authority not only through confrontation, but through ridicule. The regime's claims to moral seriousness were met with open mockery.

Crucially, the uprising transcended Tehran and other major urban centers. Protests spread to peripheral regions and ethnically diverse provinces, revealing the intersection of gender oppression with broader patterns of economic, cultural, and political exclusion. This geographic and social breadth reinforced the sense that Woman, Life, Freedom was not a narrow cultural rebellion, but a nationwide challenge to the existing order.

Repression Without Resolution

The state responded with a familiar repertoire: mass arrests, lethal force, and information suppression. Yet despite the intensity of repression, the uprising did not collapse into silence. Protests resurfaced in cycles, shifting in form and intensity rather than disappearing altogether.

What distinguished the crackdown of 2022 was not only its severity, but its declining effectiveness. Fear no longer functioned as a reliable instrument of control. The shock value of violence had already been exhausted in 2019. Instead of restoring order, repression often generated renewed defiance—particularly among those who saw no conceivable future within the system.

The regime's narrative strategies also faltered. Accusations of foreign orchestration rang hollow in the face of lived experience. The gap between official discourse and social reality widened further, eroding the state's ability to frame events on its own terms.

From Uprising to Everyday Defiance

As street protests ebbed and flowed, the deeper impact of Woman, Life, Freedom became increasingly visible in everyday life. Acts of noncompliance multiplied. Mandatory dress codes were openly ignored. Social norms imposed by the state were renegotiated in public spaces. Resistance became routine rather than exceptional.

This shift signaled a transformation in the nature of opposition. Protest was no longer confined to moments of mass mobilization. It became embedded in daily behavior, gradually undermining the regime's capacity to enforce ideological conformity.

The state could disperse crowds, but it struggled to police an entire society's conduct. Enforcement costs rose, while compliance declined. Control persisted, but authority eroded.

An Ideological Crisis Exposed

The significance of the 2022 uprising lies in the ideological vacuum it revealed. The Islamic Republic had long justified its rule through a fusion of religion, revolution, and moral order. Woman, Life, Freedom exposed the exhaustion of that framework. A growing segment of society no longer recognized its claims as legitimate, persuasive, or binding.

This loss is not easily reversed. Ideological authority, once eroded, cannot be restored through force alone. Each act of repression reinforced the perception that the regime governed not by conviction or consent, but by coercion.

The uprising did not overthrow the system. But it irreversibly altered the terrain of contention. It demonstrated that opposition had moved beyond demands for reform or relief and toward a rejection of the regime's foundational premises.

The next chapter examines what followed this rupture. After 2022, Iran did not return to "normal." Instead, dissent fragmented into persistent, decentralized forms—labor strikes, local protests, and everyday acts of defiance. What emerged was a society that appeared quieter on the surface, but was more deeply alienated from power than ever before.

Chapter 7

Fragmented but Persistent Protests (2023–2025): A Society That Remembers

In the aftermath of the Woman, Life, Freedom uprising, a familiar narrative reemerged among state officials and some external observers: the streets had quieted, the protests had failed, and order had been restored. Mass demonstrations became less visible, large crowds receded from city centers, and the apparatus of repression appeared to have regained control. Yet this apparent calm masked a deeper transformation. What followed 2022 was not a return to stability, but the consolidation of a new phase of contention—one defined by continuity rather than eruption. Protest did not disappear. It dispersed.

From Uprising to Continuity

Earlier cycles of unrest in Iran had followed a recognizable pattern: explosion, repression, silence. After 2022, that cycle fractured. Instead of a single nationwide movement, dissent diffused across social sectors and geographic spaces. Teachers, oil and gas workers, factory laborers, retirees, nurses, and municipal employees engaged in repeated strikes and demonstrations. These actions were often localized and issue-specific, sometimes short-lived—but they were persistent.

Each protest, viewed in isolation, appeared limited. Taken together, they formed a sustained pattern of pressure that tested the state's capacity to respond. The regime was no longer confronting a singular adversary or a unified movement. It faced a society that resisted intermittently, in multiple places, for multiple reasons—without waiting for permission or leadership.

This shift mattered. It deprived the state of the clarity that comes with centralized opposition and replaced it with a diffuse challenge that was harder to predict, contain, or conclusively defeat.

Politics After Illusion

Politically, the years following 2022 were defined by the collapse of belief in institutional remedies. Elections continued, but participation rates fell sharply—not as an expression of apathy, but of disengagement. The cumulative memory of 2009, 2019, and 2022 had stripped electoral politics of credibility as a pathway to change.

This loss of faith did not produce passivity. It redirected political energy away from formal institutions toward arenas that lay beyond the state's carefully managed frameworks. Protest became pragmatic rather than visionary. Demands focused on wages, pensions, working conditions, and basic dignity. Yet these demands were not naïve. They were grounded in a sober understanding: the system was neither responsive nor reformable.

The absence of illusion proved consequential. Unlike earlier movements, these protests did not expect concessions to lead to systemic change. Their objectives were defensive—slowing deterioration, resisting further loss—rather than transformative. This realism made them more difficult to neutralize through promises, symbolic gestures, or partial reforms.

Everyday Resistance as a Social Condition

Alongside organized labor actions, everyday forms of noncompliance expanded. Mandatory dress codes were openly defied. Moral policing was routinely challenged or ignored. State authority was increasingly contested in ordinary interactions—on the street, in workplaces, and in public institutions.

These acts rarely produced dramatic images or headlines. Yet they steadily eroded the regime's capacity to enforce ideological conformity. Compliance became selective, negotiated, or performative. The rules remained on the books, but their social authority weakened.

For the state, this posed a structural dilemma. Suppressing a single protest was feasible. Policing the behavior of an entire society was not. Enforcement costs rose, while returns diminished. Control persisted, but it became more labor-intensive and less reliable.

Economic Pressure and Institutional Exhaustion

The period from 2023 to 2025 unfolded against a backdrop of persistent economic crisis. Inflation remained high, the national currency continued to depreciate, and public services deteriorated. These pressures intensified labor unrest and expanded the pool of discontented citizens.

For the regime, managing this unrest became an exercise in endurance rather than governance. Security forces, courts, and administrative bodies were locked into continuous crisis management. Repression was applied repeatedly, but without the dramatic deterrent effect it once had. Each intervention consumed resources, generated resentment, and failed to address underlying causes.

This produced a condition of institutional fatigue. The state could still repress, but it could no longer stabilize. Decision-making became reactive and short-term. Long-term planning gave way to damage control. Governance drifted further from society's needs.

Memory as a Political Force

Perhaps the defining feature of this period was the role of collective memory. Iranian society had learned from experience. November 2019 had revealed the price of protest. Woman, Life, Freedom had demonstrated the possibility—and limits—of sustained defiance. These memories reshaped expectations on both sides of the conflict.

Protesters calibrated their actions with a clear understanding of risk, avoiding total retreat without embracing reckless confrontation. The state, in turn, operated with a mixture of aggression and caution, aware that unrestrained violence could provoke wider backlash.

Memory thus functioned as a political force. It connected fragmented acts of resistance into a coherent historical process, even in the absence of centralized leadership or ideology. What appeared scattered on the surface was unified beneath by shared experience.

The Limits of Control

By the mid-2020s, the Islamic Republic confronted a familiar paradox in a new form. It had prevented another nationwide uprising—at least temporarily—but only by normalizing low-level conflict across society. Control was maintained, but stability remained elusive.

This phase revealed the structural limits of repression as a governing strategy. Suppression could delay confrontation, but it could not restore legitimacy or trust. Each unresolved grievance added to a growing reservoir of social strain. The society that emerged from this period was quieter, but not reconciled. It was fragmented, but not defeated. It remembered—and that memory shaped every encounter with power.

The next chapter steps back from the chronology of protests to examine repression itself as a governing strategy. How did an instrument once used to manage crises become the regime's default mode of rule—and why did that transformation lead not to stability, but to permanent vulnerability?

Chapter 8

Repression as Strategy: From Temporary Tool to Permanent Dead End

In the Islamic Republic, repression did not originate as a comprehensive doctrine of governance. In its early decades, coercion was framed as an exceptional response—justified by revolution, war, and the language of existential threat. Over time, however, repression ceased to be episodic. It hardened into the regime's default strategy for managing society. What began as a tool gradually became a system.

This transformation was not abrupt. It unfolded through a series of decisions taken at moments of crisis. Each time the state confronted organized dissent—students in 1999, voters in 2009, marginalized communities in 2017, economically desperate protesters in 2019, and a society rejecting ideological control in 2022—it chose force over accommodation. Each choice appeared rational in the short term. Order was restored. The streets were cleared. The system survived. But survival came at a cumulative cost that steadily narrowed the regime's future options.

The Logic of Short-Term Control

Repression is effective in one narrow sense: it can rapidly disrupt collective action. By arresting leaders, intimidating participants, fragmenting networks, and monopolizing narratives, an authoritarian state can buy time. In Iran, this logic guided responses across successive waves of protest. Each crackdown seemed to confirm the efficacy of force.

Yet repression solves only the problem it is designed to see. It treats dissent as a security threat rather than as a social signal. Grievances are not addressed; they are deferred. Each act of suppression pushes unresolved tensions into the future, where they return under altered—and often more volatile—conditions. Over time, the state becomes trapped by its own apparent success. Having relied on coercion to restore order, it must continue to do so, because alternative mechanisms—dialogue, reform, compromise—have been systematically dismantled or discredited.

The Expansion of the Security Lens

As repression hardened into strategy, the security lens expanded to encompass nearly every domain of governance. Economic policy, labor relations, cultural expression, environmental activism, and even public health debates were increasingly framed as matters of national security. Ordinary social problems were reclassified as existential threats.

The consequences were profound. When every issue is treated as a security concern, policymaking becomes rigid and reactive. Flexibility is perceived as weakness. Transparency becomes risky. Expertise yields to loyalty. Institutions tasked with governance are subordinated to institutions tasked with control. This shift did not strengthen the state's capacity to rule. It hollowed it out.

Repression and the Erosion of Trust

Sustained repression carries a social cost that accumulates silently: the erosion of trust. In Iran, repeated crackdowns taught citizens that engagement carried risk without reward. Participation in elections, civic organizations, unions, or public debate increasingly appeared futile—or dangerous.

As trust eroded, so did the regime's ability to communicate with society. Even when authorities attempted limited reforms or concessions, these gestures were met with skepticism. Collective memory intervened. Past repression reframed present offers as tactical rather than sincere. A feedback loop emerged. Distrust fueled disengagement or protest. Protest triggered repression. Repression deepened distrust. Over time, the state lost not only legitimacy, but intelligibility. It continued to speak, but fewer believed.

Institutional Consequences and Adaptive Resistance

The turn toward repression reshaped the state from within. Security and judicial institutions expanded in power and reach, while technocratic and representative bodies declined. Decision-making centralized, accountability diminished, and policy horizons shortened. Institutions designed for coercion crowded out those designed for problem-solving.

This imbalance weakened governance. Bodies optimized for enforcement proved ill-suited to manage complex social and economic challenges. As repression absorbed more resources and attention, crises multiplied—and each new crisis reinforced reliance on the same failing strategy.

Seeing this, society adapted. Protesters learned to operate without leaders, to disperse quickly, to embed resistance in everyday life, and to calibrate risk with memory. Fear lost its paralyzing force. The cost of control rose; its returns diminished.

From Crisis Management to Permanent Condition

By the mid-2020s, repression had become a permanent condition rather than a temporary response. The regime could no longer imagine governing without it. Yet this permanence revealed a paradox: a system dependent on constant coercion is inherently unstable.

Each act of repression undermined the possibility of political recovery. Each crackdown narrowed the space for compromise. Power was preserved, but resilience was consumed. What remained was a state capable of force, yet increasingly incapable of governance. This is the dead end repression produces. It eliminates alternatives without offering a viable path forward. It sustains the present by mortgaging the future.

The chapters that follow turn inward, examining how this strategic impasse manifested within the regime's own institutions— how bodies designed to ensure stability instead generated dysfunction and self-erosion. Understanding this internal unraveling is essential to grasping why repeated repression did not avert collapse, but made it more likely.

Chapter 9

The Evolution of Repression: From Containment to the Normalization of Lethal Force

Understanding Iran's protest movements without examining the evolution of state repression produces an incomplete picture. Over the past four decades, the Islamic Republic has not merely repeated patterns of suppression; it has learned from each confrontation, refined its coercive tools, and institutionalized violence as a governing practice. Each wave of protest has served as a testing ground—allowing the state to measure social tolerance, international reaction, and the effectiveness of brutality as a deterrent. This chapter traces how repression itself became cumulative, increasingly lethal, and ultimately self-defeating.

Changing Modes of Repression: From Security Control to Survival at Any Cost

During the 1999 student uprising, repression still operated within a limited, reactive framework. The violent raid on Tehran University dormitories, targeted arrests of student leaders, and pressure on reformist media reflected a state attempting to restore order, not annihilate dissent. Excessive force was often explained as the work of "rogue elements" rather than official policy.

The 2009 Green Movement marked a structural shift. Faced with mass demonstrations directly challenging electoral legitimacy, the

63

regime responded with a coordinated strategy: street violence, mass arrests, televised forced confessions, show trials, and media censorship. Repression ceased to be episodic; it became an instrument of governance.

A further transformation occurred after December 2017, when protests spread beyond major cities into economically marginalized regions. The state increasingly abandoned calibrated force in favor of preemptive and lethal suppression. This trajectory reached its clearest expression in November 2019, when security forces used live ammunition at scale and imposed a near-total internet blackout.

By the time of the 2022 uprising and the nationwide protests of 2025–2026, repression resembled a form of low-intensity internal warfare. The objective was no longer control, but deterrence through terror.

Comparative Data: Escalating Killings, Arrests, and Executions

Data compiled by international human rights organizations and UN mechanisms reveal a consistent pattern: each protest cycle produced higher levels of violence.

Table 1 – Comparative Scale of Repression Across Protest Waves

PROTEST WAVE	ESTIMATED DEATHS	ARRESTS	USE OF EXECUTIONS
1999	Dozens	Hundreds	No
2009	Dozens	Thousands	No
2017–2018	Dozens	Thousands	Rare
2019	Hundreds–1,000+	Tens of thousands	Post-protest
2022	Hundreds (incl. minors)	Thousands	Yes
2025–2026	Thousands (est.)	Tens of thousands	Systematic

While precise figures vary due to state opacity, the trend is unmistakable: repression in Iran has become progressively more lethal, more indiscriminate, and more punitive.

The Escalation of Brutality: From Controlled Force to Open Cruelty

Earlier protest responses attempted to maintain a degree of plausible deniability. Over time, this restraint disappeared. Reports increasingly document:

- Direct gunfire aimed at heads and chests
- Use of birdshot and military-grade ammunition
- Fatal beatings and torture in detention
- Denial of medical care to wounded protesters
- Raids on hospitals and arrests of injured demonstrators

Cruelty ceased to be exceptional. It became normalized—an everyday feature of state response. This shift reflects the erosion of internal ethical constraints and their replacement with a governing logic rooted entirely in fear.

Defining Moments in Each Protest Cycle

Each uprising produced critical events that reshaped both protest and repression:

Table 2 – Turning Points in Iran's Protest Cycles

YEAR	DEFINING EVENT
1999	Assault on Tehran University dormitories
2009	Killing of Neda Agha-Soltan; house arrest of leaders
2017	Spread to small and peripheral cities
2019	Nationwide internet shutdown; mass killings
2022	Death of Mahsa Amini; women-led resistance
2025–2026	Economic collapse + strikes + nationwide revolt + mass killing

These moments altered expectations, shattered taboos, and recalibrated both state violence and social resistance.

Plainclothes Forces: Violence Without Accountability

The increasing reliance on plainclothes operatives—often linked to Basij or intelligence networks—has been central to the regime's repression strategy. Initially auxiliary, these forces evolved into the backbone of street-level violence, enabling:

- Denial of responsibility
- Blurred lines between civilians and security forces
- Arbitrary and anonymous brutality

By the latest protest waves, the distinction between formal and informal repression had effectively collapsed.

Labeling, Polarization, and the Manufacture of Legitimacy

Across protest cycles, the regime has relied on discursive warfare to justify violence. Protesters were progressively redefined:

- "Rioters" instead of citizens
- "Foreign agents" instead of dissenters
- "Terrorists" instead of demonstrators
- "Morally corrupt" instead of women resisting compulsion

This language performs a crucial function: it dehumanizes protesters, lowering the psychological threshold for killing and mass punishment.

International Attention: Rising Visibility, Limited Deterrence

Over time, international attention to protests and repression in Iran has increased markedly. Compared to the early decades of the Islamic Republic, human rights violations—particularly those linked to the suppression of protest movements—are now far more visible in global forums. This heightened attention has culminated in repeated resolutions by the United Nations Human Rights Council, the establishment of fact-finding mechanisms,[21] regular reporting by Special Rapporteurs,[22] and coordinated condemnations by states and

---

[21] Independent International Fact-Finding Mission on Iran — In response to widespread allegations of serious human rights violations by Iranian authorities during the nationwide Woman, Life, Freedom protests that began in September 2022, the United Nations Human Rights Council adopted a landmark resolution on 24 November 2022, establishing an Independent International Fact-Finding Mission on the Islamic Republic of Iran to investigate and document alleged abuses, with a particular focus on violations against women and children. The mission's mandate was to collect, analyze, record, and preserve evidence of violations that may amount to crimes under international law and to report findings back to the Council. In subsequent years, the Council extended and broadened the mission's mandate (notably in April 2025) to investigate not only violations from the 2022 protests but recent and ongoing serious human rights violations, with the aim of enabling future legal proceedings and accountability efforts. Iran has consistently denied access to the mission and Special Rapporteurs, but the body has issued detailed reports concluding that violations—including killings, torture, and sexual violence—likely amount to crimes against humanity.

[22] Special Rapporteur on the situation of human rights in the Islamic Republic of Iran — The United Nations Human Rights Council, recognizing persistent and widespread human rights violations in Iran, re-established the mandate of a Special Rapporteur on the human rights situation in the country on 24 March 2011 to monitor, investigate, and report on abuses and to engage with the Iranian government and other stakeholders. The mandate requires the Special Rapporteur to document ongoing violations, issue urgent appeals, and submit regular reports to the Human Rights Council and the UN General Assembly, although Iran has consistently denied access to the mandate-holder. Over time, successive Special Rapporteurs—including Ahmed Shaheed (2011–2016), Javaid Rehman (2018–2024), and the current mandate-holder Mai Sato (from August 2024)—have produced annual and thematic reports detailing violations of civil, political,

international institutions. Yet despite this growing visibility, international scrutiny has rarely translated into effective deterrence of state violence.

A central factor shaping this outcome has been the Islamic Republic's systematic refusal to grant access to international human rights monitors. Since the creation of the UN Special Rapporteur mandate on the situation of human rights in Iran, Iranian authorities have consistently denied entry to mandate holders. This policy—maintained without interruption across different administrations—forms a core element of the regime's strategy to control narratives, prevent independent on-the-ground investigation, and minimize the international costs of repression. By barring direct access, the state has sought to shield itself from first-hand documentation, unrestricted interviews with victims, and independent verification of abuses.

However, the absence of official access has not meant the absence of documentation. On the contrary, one of the defining features of protest cycles in Iran—particularly since 2009—has been the expanding role of civil society networks, human rights organizations, citizen journalists, and activists, both inside and outside the country, in documenting violations. Iranian and international human rights groups have relied on survivor testimony, visual evidence, medical records, court documents, and accounts from families of victims to reconstruct events with remarkable detail. These decentralized documentation efforts have played a decisive

---

economic, and social rights, including the use of excessive force against peaceful protesters, arbitrary detention, and discrimination against women and minorities. Despite repeated recommendations and urgent appeals from the Special Rapporteur, the Iranian government's refusal to cooperate or allow country visits has limited the direct impact of these reports on the ground, even as they have shaped international awareness and pressure on the human rights situation in Iran.

role in bringing Iran's human rights situation to sustained international attention.

In this sense, international scrutiny of repression in Iran has largely developed from the bottom up rather than from the top down. It was the accumulation of civil documentation—often produced under extreme risk and amid internet shutdowns—that enabled UN bodies to issue detailed reports, justify the creation of investigative mechanisms, and maintain Iran on the international human rights agenda. Without these informal yet extensive documentation networks, many episodes of violence—particularly those occurring during periods of information blackout—would likely have remained invisible beyond Iran's borders.

At the same time, the role of the United Nations has remained constrained by structural limitations. The UN possesses tools to monitor, document, and report violations, but it lacks direct enforcement mechanisms capable of halting repression in real time. Human rights resolutions are non-binding, reports are often retrospective, and pathways to international criminal accountability face substantial legal and political obstacles. Geopolitical fragmentation, competing global priorities, and divergent state interests have further weakened the consistency and impact of international responses.

Iranian authorities, for their part, have learned to absorb and manage international pressure. Through repeated internet shutdowns, tight control over domestic media, and a long-standing practice of dismissing external criticism as politicized interference, the regime has limited the practical consequences of global condemnation. In many instances, repression has not diminished in response to international attention; instead, it has intensified, suggesting that the state continues to view internal dissent as a far greater threat to its survival than external reputational costs.

The Iranian case thus highlights a fundamental paradox of the international human rights system: greater visibility does not automatically produce greater restraint. Documentation, reporting, and global awareness have succeeded in challenging official narratives and creating an international record of abuse, but they have not, on their own, been sufficient to disrupt the cycle of violence. The gap between knowledge and action—between exposure and accountability—remains one of the central tensions in the international response to systematic repression, and nowhere is this more evident than in Iran.

Repression as a Pathway to Systemic Exhaustion

This comparative analysis reveals a central paradox: the more violently the state suppressed dissent, the more deeply rooted and radicalized resistance became. Repression, once a tool of survival, transformed into a mechanism of permanent crisis.

The Islamic Republic did not come to the edge of collapse because it failed to repress. It approaches collapse because repression became its only language of governance.

Chapter 10

Institutional Self-Erosion: When the State Consumes Itself

Authoritarian systems often endure by constructing institutions capable of both governance and coercion. In the Islamic Republic, these institutions were never merely administrative. They were designed to embody revolutionary legitimacy, enforce order, and guarantee continuity. Yet as repression hardened into a permanent strategy, the very institutions built to preserve the system began to erode from within. Institution-building gradually gave way to institutional self-consumption.

This erosion was not triggered by a single failure or shock. It was the cumulative outcome of a governance model that consistently prioritized control over competence and loyalty over legitimacy. Over time, the structures meant to stabilize the system became impediments to its effective operation.

The Expansion—and Deformation—of Power

One of the most visible expressions of institutional self-erosion was the expansion of security and military bodies into domains far beyond their original mandates. The Islamic Revolutionary Guard Corps, initially established as a revolutionary force and later

71

consolidated as a military institution, evolved into a dominant political and economic actor.

This expansion was not guided by transparent planning or functional specialization. It followed a logic of trust. As civilian institutions lost autonomy and credibility, power gravitated toward bodies deemed ideologically reliable. Economic projects, infrastructure contracts, media outlets, and cultural initiatives were absorbed into security-linked networks.

In the short term, this consolidation appeared to strengthen control. In the long term, it deformed governance. Institutional boundaries blurred. Conflicts of interest multiplied. Bodies tasked with enforcing order became stakeholders in the very economic arrangements that produced social discontent. Accountability weakened, efficiency declined, and public resentment deepened.

Law as Instrument—and the Cost of Instrumentalization

The judiciary underwent a parallel transformation. Courts increasingly functioned as instruments of political discipline rather than as arbiters of justice. Protesters, journalists, labor organizers, and civil society actors were prosecuted under expansive national security charges through opaque procedures.

While these practices delivered immediate deterrence, they inflicted lasting damage on the institution itself. As legal processes became visibly politicized, public confidence collapsed. Law lost its normative authority and came to be understood as an extension of coercion.

This erosion had systemic consequences. When courts are perceived as tools of power rather than forums for redress, disputes migrate outside legal channels. Informal resistance, evasion, and confrontation replace institutional mediation—further destabilizing governance and increasing reliance on force.

Media, Narrative, and the Breakdown of Persuasion

State-affiliated media experienced a similar decay. Once intended to communicate the regime's vision and maintain public engagement, they increasingly served as vehicles for denial and distortion. Major crises were downplayed, casualties ignored, and dissent delegitimized.

This approach did more than fail to persuade; it severed communication. Large segments of society disengaged from official media altogether, turning instead to external sources and informal networks. The state retained the capacity to broadcast, but lost the ability to convince.

Narrative control—long a pillar of authoritarian stability—thus weakened. The state continued to speak, but fewer listened. Each crisis widened the gap between lived experience and official representation, accelerating the loss of institutional relevance.

Internal Degradation and Decision Paralysis

Institutional self-erosion was not confined to public perception. It reshaped internal dynamics as well. As loyalty became the primary criterion for advancement, expertise and initiative were sidelined. Decision-making grew risk-averse, short-term, and defensive.

Bureaucrats learned that avoiding responsibility was safer than solving problems. Policies were crafted to minimize immediate political risk rather than address structural challenges. The result was a culture of inertia: constant directives, meetings, and enforcement actions that produced the appearance of activity while hollowing out functionality.

This dynamic intensified during the post-2022 period. Institutions were forced into perpetual crisis management, reacting to labor unrest, economic instability, and social defiance without the capacity to prevent recurrence. The state functioned, but without direction.

The Paradox of Strength

By the mid-2020s, the Islamic Republic confronted a paradox. Its institutions appeared powerful—armed, expansive, and deeply embedded in society—yet they were increasingly incapable of effective governance. The more authority they accumulated, the less trust they commanded. The more they intervened, the more resistance they generated.

This paradox explains why omnipresent repression failed to restore stability. Institutions optimized for enforcement could not generate legitimacy. Institutions nominally responsible for governance had been subordinated to security imperatives they were ill-equipped to manage.

The state had not collapsed. But it had entered a condition of chronic institutional fragility—one in which survival depended on constant exertion and crisis management rather than adaptability and consent.

Self-Erosion as a Path to Collapse

Institutional self-erosion rarely produces dramatic endings. It produces prolonged vulnerability. Systems continue to operate, but at rising cost and diminishing resilience. Each shock—economic, social, or political—extracts a greater toll than the last.

In this condition, collapse becomes a process rather than an event. It unfolds through cumulative dysfunction, waning legitimacy, and the steady exhaustion of governing capacity. Repression may delay reckoning, but it cannot reverse trajectory.

The next chapter draws these strands together. It explains why each successive crackdown—rather than securing the regime's future—brought its unraveling closer, and why the path the Islamic Republic chose ultimately left it with fewer exits at every turn.

Chapter 11

Why Every Crackdown Brought Collapse Closer

When viewed in isolation, each episode of repression in the Islamic Republic appeared to achieve its immediate objective. Protests were dispersed, organizers neutralized, and order—at least on the surface—restored. Yet when these crackdowns are examined not as discrete incidents but as a cumulative sequence, a different logic becomes visible. Each act of repression resolved a short-term challenge while deepening the structural conditions that produced the next one. Over time, repression ceased to function as a stabilizing response and instead became a mechanism of acceleration.

The first casualty of repeated crackdowns was the possibility of internal correction. The suppression of the student uprising in 1999 demonstrated that even limited, reformist demands could provoke violence. The crushing of the Green Movement in 2009 extended this lesson to the electoral arena, stripping elections of their credibility as vehicles for meaningful change. Each crackdown closed a channel through which social pressure might have been absorbed, redirected, or negotiated. What remained was a narrowing corridor of options in which confrontation became increasingly likely.

As institutional pathways were sealed, repression began to exact a cumulative toll on legitimacy. Legitimacy is not an abstract moral attribute; it is a practical resource that allows states to govern with fewer coercive inputs and greater social compliance. With each violent intervention, the Islamic Republic depleted this resource. November 2019 marked a decisive threshold in this process. The deployment of mass lethal force against unarmed protesters preserved control in the immediate sense, but it irreversibly damaged the regime's moral standing. Consent was not merely weakened; it was forfeited.

The erosion of legitimacy was accompanied by the breakdown of a shared political language. Even authoritarian systems depend on some degree of communicative exchange between rulers and ruled—signals that grievances are heard, promises that participation matters, and narratives that make governance intelligible. Repression systematically dismantled this exchange. Protesters learned that engagement carried risk without reward, while authorities increasingly interpreted dissent exclusively through a security lens. Dialogue gave way to suspicion; policy to force.

This breakdown reshaped the social composition of dissent. Early protest movements were dominated by students and urban middle classes who sought reform within the system's existing framework. Their suppression pushed contention outward—to economically marginalized communities, peripheral regions, and groups with little investment in institutional politics. The protests of 2017 and the uprising of November 2019 reflected this shift. These movements were driven less by political ideals than by survival. They were harder to co-opt, less predictable, and more volatile.

Repression also carried economic consequences that compounded the crisis. As institutions devoted growing resources to surveillance, enforcement, and punishment, their capacity to address structural economic challenges declined. Corruption intensified, inequality widened, and mismanagement deepened. Economic grievances multiplied, generating new waves of discontent that repression could neither resolve nor sustainably contain. Each crisis fed the next, producing a cycle in which scarcity and unrest reinforced one another.

Crucially, repression failed to sustain fear as a durable instrument of governance. Fear can immobilize populations temporarily, but when it is repeatedly experienced without relief or resolution, it transforms. In Iran, fear evolved into resignation for some, but into defiance for others. The Woman, Life, Freedom uprising of 2022 revealed this transformation with clarity. Protesters confronted the state fully aware of the risks, indicating that the deterrent power of violence had diminished. Repression no longer shocked; it confirmed.

By the mid-2020s, the regime found itself caught in a strategic trap of its own making. Having relied on repression to survive successive crises, it could no longer pivot to alternative modes of governance. Concessions risked being read as weakness; further repression deepened alienation. Stability became more costly to maintain and more fragile in effect.

This dynamic explains why each crackdown brought collapse closer rather than pushing it further away. Repression preserved the present by mortgaging the future. It eliminated immediate threats at the expense of long-term resilience. With each cycle, the margin for error narrowed, and the consequences of miscalculation grew more severe.

Collapse, in this sense, is not a single dramatic moment. It is the accumulation of lost opportunities, depleted legitimacy, and exhausted institutions. The Islamic Republic did not move toward collapse despite its reliance on repression, but because of it.

The final chapter steps back to consider what this trajectory reveals about authoritarian durability and decline. It reframes collapse not as an abrupt rupture, but as a process—one produced through repetition, erosion, and the steady exhaustion of a system's capacity to adapt.

Chapter 12

Collapse as a Process, Not an Event

When political systems collapse, they are often remembered through images of sudden rupture: a decisive uprising, a dramatic fall, a single moment that marks the end. Yet the trajectory traced in this book points to a different reality. In the case of the Islamic Republic, collapse is better understood not as an event, but as a process—gradual, cumulative, and shaped by a long series of choices made in response to dissent.

From the aftermath of the Iran–Iraq War to the protests of December 2025 and January 2026, the regime's response to social pressure followed a remarkably consistent logic. Faced with demands for change, it chose repression over reform, control over negotiation, and short-term survival over long-term legitimacy. Each decision appeared rational in isolation. Each preserved power in the moment. Taken together, however, they produced a trajectory of erosion that steadily undermined the foundations of governance.

This book has shown how that erosion unfolded across interconnected dimensions. Politically, successive crackdowns dismantled every credible mechanism for internal correction. The suppression of student protests revealed the limits of reform. The crushing of the Green Movement destroyed the credibility of elections as instruments of change. Later uprisings demonstrated that neither ballots nor institutional participation offered meaningful pathways forward. As these channels closed, politics migrated outward—from formal arenas to the streets, and eventually into diffuse, everyday forms of resistance.

Socially, repression reshaped both the composition and the meaning of dissent. Early movements led by students and urban middle classes gave way to protests driven by economic survival, identity, and dignity. Each wave expanded the circle of alienation. By the time Woman, Life, Freedom erupted in 2022, opposition was no longer framed as disappointment with the system, but as estrangement from it. The state no longer confronted citizens seeking inclusion; it faced a society increasingly unwilling to recognize its authority.

Economically, the securitization of dissent diverted attention and resources away from structural reform. Inequality deepened, public services deteriorated, and corruption hardened into a governing norm. Repression became the primary means of managing the symptoms of economic failure, while the underlying causes intensified. Scarcity and discontent reinforced one another in a cycle that coercion could not break.

Institutionally, the permanent turn toward repression hollowed out the state itself. Bodies designed to govern were subordinated to those designed to control. Expertise yielded to loyalty, accountability to obedience. Over time, institutions lost not only public trust, but internal capacity. The state became increasingly adept at enforcing order—and increasingly incapable of solving problems.

At every stage, repression bought time. But time was purchased at a growing price. Legitimacy was consumed, trust depleted, and resilience exhausted. The regime survived, but it did so by drawing down the very resources that make survival sustainable.

This is the paradox at the heart of authoritarian durability: the strategies that secure short-term control often undermine long-term stability. The Islamic Republic's reliance on repression did not postpone collapse indefinitely; it transformed collapse into a prolonged condition of vulnerability—one in which each new crisis carried higher stakes and fewer exits.

The protests of December 2025 and January 2026, described at the opening of this book, did not mark the end of this process. They illuminated its advanced stage. Society returned to the streets not with illusions of reform, but with the clarity born of experience. The state responded not with persuasion or accommodation, but with familiar force. What had changed was not the method of rule, but its diminishing effectiveness.

This book does not predict when or how the Islamic Republic will fall. History rarely grants such certainty. What it does demonstrate is that the system has entered a phase in which collapse is no longer contingent on a single shock. It is embedded in the cumulative effects of past decisions—in the narrowing of options, the exhaustion of institutions, and the erosion of consent.

Understanding collapse as a process rather than an event allows us to see continuity where others see repetition, and inevitability where others see surprise. It explains why each uprising, even when suppressed, matters—not because it succeeds immediately, but because it leaves behind a transformed society and a weakened state.

The Islamic Republic did not move toward collapse because it failed to repress dissent. It moved toward collapse because repression became its defining mode of governance.

In that sense, the story told in these pages is not only about Iran. It is about the limits of authoritarian control, the costs of ruling through fear, and the ways in which power can survive crisis after crisis while steadily hollowing itself out.

Collapse, when it comes, will not be the result of a single protest or a single decision. It will be the outcome of a long journey—one the regime has already been traveling for decades.

About the Author

Roozbeh Mirebrahimi is an Iranian journalist, researcher, and author whose work focuses on political power, authoritarian institutions, and social movements in contemporary Iran. With more than two decades of experience in journalism and political analysis, his writing bridges investigative reporting, historical inquiry, and long-form analytical narrative.

Mirebrahimi has written extensively on the evolution of the Islamic Republic's political structure, with particular attention to the relationship between repression, law, and institutional power. His previous books include *The First Brick: How Revolution Gave Birth to Theocracy in Iran,* a study of the early constitutional and ideological foundations of the post-1979 system; *Guardian of Authoritarianism,* an in-depth examination of the Guardian Council's role in preserving clerical rule; and *The Grip on Power in the Cloak of Law*, which traces the institutionalization of the Islamic Revolutionary Guard Corps through legal and political mechanisms.

In addition to his books, Mirebrahimi has contributed analysis and reporting to Persian-language and international media, and has collaborated with civil society organizations and human rights initiatives documenting state repression in Iran. His work often draws on a combination of archival research, legal analysis, and lived observation of Iran's political transformations.

Why Iran Is Unraveling; Protest, Repression, and the Crisis of Power brings together years of research and reflection on Iran's protest movements and the state's response to them. Rather than treating collapse as a sudden rupture, Mirebrahimi examines it as a cumulative process—shaped by repeated choices to suppress dissent and the long-term consequences of governing through force.

Index

1

2

A

B

C

D

E

G

www.ingramcontent.com/pod-product-compliance
Lightning Source LLC
Chambersburg PA
CBHW032209040426
42449CB00005B/501